Flaxseed Recipes

How to use flaxseed in omega 3, low carb, wheat free, egg free, celiac disease and gluten free recipes. Includes 36 flax seed recipes

Ellen Vincent

© 2013 by *Ellen Vincent*

All Rights Reserved. No part of this publication may be reproduced in any form or by any means, including scanning, photocopying, or otherwise without prior written permission of the copyright holder.

Disclaimer and Terms of Use: The Author and Publisher has strived to be as accurate and complete as possible in the creation of this book, notwithstanding the fact that she does not warrant or represent at any time that the contents within are accurate due to the rapidly changing nature of science and medicine. While all attempts have been made to verify information provided in this publication, the Author and Publisher assumes no responsibility for errors, omissions, or contrary interpretation of the subject matter herein. Any perceived slights of specific persons, peoples, or organizations are unintentional. In practical advice books, like anything else in life, there are no guarantees of any results obtained. Readers are cautioned to rely on their own judgment and seek professional medical advice about their individual circumstances and to act accordingly.

First Printing, 2013

ISBN -13: 978-1493606641

ISBN -10: 1493606646

Printed in the United States of America

Dedication

For Titus

Flaxseed Recipes

How to use flaxseed in omega 3, low carb, wheat free, egg free, celiac disease and gluten free recipes. Includes 36 flax seed recipes

Table of Contents

Introduction 9
Flax Seeds for Omega 3 Fatty Acids 13
You Can Add Flaxseed in a Number of Different Ways .. 19
Flaxseed as a Substitute 25
Making Flaxseed Gel 33
Low Carb Diets and Flaxseed 35
Help with Coeliac Disease 37
Flaxseed Recipes 41
   Getting the Main Ingredients 41
   Banana Flax Bread 42
   Oatmeal Bran and Flax Meal Muffins 43
   Cheesy Flaxseed Breaded Chicken Breast 45
   Flaxseed Low Carb and Gluten Free Bread 47
   Flaxseed Low Carb and Gluten Free Pizza Base 49
   Strawberry and Flaxseed Smoothie 51
   Granola with Flaxseed 52
   Cinnamon Muffins 53
   Apple Pecan Muffins 54
   Low Carb Blueberry and Walnut Muffins 55
   Low Carb Duffins 57
   Low Carb Cheesy Crackers 59
   Low Carb Breakfast Cereal 60
   Low Carb Breakfast Smoothie 61
   Almond and Flaxseed Gluten Free Bread 62
   Flaxseed and Cashew Nut Energy Bar 63
   Quick and Easy Cookies 65
   Vegetable and Flaxseed Fritters 66
   Quick and Easy Low Carb Flaxseed Wraps 68
   Flaxseed Bread Made in a Bread Machine 69
   Flaxseed and Wholemeal Flour Pancakes 70
   Flaxseed Raita 72
   Fig and Flaxseed Biscuits 73
   Low Carb Flaxseed Crisp Thins 74

Flaxseed Waffles.. 76
Vegan Flaxseed and Nut Meat Loaf 77
Flaxseed and Almond Burgers 79
Flaxseed and Hot Pepper Smoothie..............................80
Flaxseed and Chilli Corn Bread.....................................81
Flaxseed Savoury Slice 83
Flaxseed and Greek Yoghurt 84
Flaxseed Tea 85
Flaxseed and Whole Grain Rice 86
Flaxseed Oil Salad Dressing 87
Flaxseed Muesli 88
Conclusion...91
About the Author 93

Introduction

Flaxseeds before harvest

Flax seeds contain lots of good ingredients, such as omega 3 fats, that would be good to include in our day to day diets. This book is dedicated to showing you how you can include more flax seeds in the recipes that you cook. Sometimes it will just be a case of adding some flaxseeds to an existing recipe. Other times it will involve substituting flax, in part or totally, for an existing ingredient in a recipe. Finally there are recipes that are designed to use flax seed as a main ingredient. Flax seeds and their contents are not usually used in most cooking. Due to the special characteristics of flax seeds you have to add them to your recipes in a careful and considered way. In this book you will gain all of the knowledge that you need in order to successfully integrate flax seeds into your diet. This will then both improve the nutrient profile of your food as well as adding some interesting flavours and textures to the food.

Despite flaxseeds only being relatively small seeds they contain lots of useful nutrients. Although they aren't classed as a grain they have a nutrient profile that is very similar. The have the same kinds of vitamins and minerals. There are lots of B vitamins as well as magnesium and manganese minerals in each seed. In a number of respects these little seeds are even better than grains such as wheat: they contain more antioxidants, omega 3 fatty acids and fibre. As well as this, flax seeds contain very low amounts of carbohydrate. This means that they are ideal for people who need to cut down the amount of carbohydrate in the form of starch and sugars that they are consuming. The low levels of carbohydrate, high levels of healthy fats and high levels of fibre make them an ideal food as part of a weight loss diet. They can also make it easier for people to keep to their ideal weight once they have reached it. The combination of healthy fats and fibre has the effect of making people feel that they are full. This then helps to reduce the cravings for food between meals. This is an ideal situation for dieters as most people find that they quit their diets due to the difficulty in keeping to the strict limits of food intake.

Flax seeds have lots of omega 3 fats, fibre and important nutrients such as lignans. They also contain naturally low amounts of saturated fats and cholesterol. This makes them a healthy choice when it comes to some recipe substitutions. As a result of providing this healthy option flax seeds are rapidly becoming very popular when it comes to recipe addition and substitution.

It may come as quite a surprise to find out that a lot of the unhealthy processed flour and unhealthy fats can be replaced with the good omega 3 fats and fibre found in flaxseeds. In addition to this adding flaxseed to baked foods can provide more texture and make the food moister as well as providing a lovely nutty flavour.

Flax seeds are naturally low in carbohydrate and as a result they can become an important part of a low carbohydrate diet. Whole flax seeds will pass through the digestive system intact and as a result you won't benefit from the nutrients within them. You have to grind the flaxseeds to make the nutrients available.

Flax Seeds for Omega 3 Fatty Acids

Flax seed has been a widely grown crop for thousands of years, and it is believed that it was one of the first plants that humans domesticated and farmed. It is one of the most versatile plants in the world, capable of being made into fabrics such as linen, medicines, high quality paper such as that used for money, soap, and all sorts of other things. The most useful thing that flax seed can be made into, however, is linseed oil, which is also known as flaxseed oil.

Golden Flaxseeds

There are 2 types of Flaxseed. These are called 'Brown' and 'Golden' Flaxseed. Brown flax, can be eaten however, it is grown for the commercial Linseed Oil, paint, and solvents Industries. The Omega Golden Flax Seed was developed for human consumption and is preferred for the food market because of its nutty buttery flavour. The nutritional value of golden flaxseed and brown flaxseed are very similar if the samples are of the same quality. Quality is very important in determining the omega 3 and omega-6 content and overall nutritional value.

You should try to choose the golden flaxseeds rather than the brown variety when it comes to baking. This is because the brown seed coats will tend to make your baked food a lot darker in colour rather than a nice pleasing golden colour. Obviously, if this isn't very important to you then it is up to you which type you use.

Brown Flaxseeds

Linseed oil is one of the most commonly used vegetable oils. As well as being used in food, it has also been used as a finish and polish for wood and painted surfaces, in putty and caulk, and perhaps most notably in linoleum, which many people wrongly believe is made from man made materials. Linoleum is actually wood or cork dust on canvas, overlaid with solidified linseed oil, making an all natural floor covering that is especially suitable for people with allergies. Wood is also treated with linseed oil when making bats for some sports, including cricket.

The popularity of linseed oil for food preparation has been steadily growing again, as people have been paying more attention to the benefits of omega-3 fatty acids, which the oil is rich in, while also being low in the omega-6 fatty acids that many people are now trying to avoid. Some have come to use it as an alternative to cod liver oil, and it is readily edible poured straight onto salads. It has a nut like flavour. If you do not like the taste, though, capsules of the oil are also available. As most of the world's flax seed is cultivated in Europe, it is much cheaper there than elsewhere, but as a rule it should be cheaper than cod liver oil in almost all countries.

Flax seeds are a good source of Omega 3 fatty acids. In addition to this flax seeds are also rich in fibre, protein, vitamins and minerals. The fibre in the flax seeds can help stabilize blood sugar levels. The seeds are a great source for protein: for every 100 grams of the flax seeds you can get about 18 grams of protein. Flax seeds also contain vitamin E and B. The seeds are also rich in zinc, iron, copper, magnesium, nickel, calcium and many other essential minerals.

There are many benefits to adding flax seeds to your diet. An example of this is where flax seeds can help with your acne problems. The presence of fatty acids in the seeds helps to control the production of androgens, which causes acne.

Golden flax can be purchased whole, ground and in oil form. It is recommended that you obtain golden flax seeds in the whole seed form as it provides the highest nutritional value. You should grind portions of your golden flax seeds as needed. The golden flax seeds can be ground into a coarse powder form using a coffee grinder or electric flax grinder. Uncrushed flax seeds will not be digested and will thus pass through you undigested. This means that you will be missing out on any Omega 3 fatty acids that they contain.

Whole golden flax seed, which is clean, dry and of good quality can be stored at room temperature for up to a year. For optimum freshness, ground flax seed should be ground as needed. This is important because they start to lose their healthy content as soon as they are ground. Unused ground flax seed can be refrigerated in an airtight container if it will be used in just a matter of days, or it can be stored in the freezer for about a month.

You should drink a lot of water after consuming flax seeds. You should also eat just the right amounts, which consists of no more then 3 tablespoons twice a day. If you exceed that by large amounts it can cause a toxic effect. As a result you should be careful.

There are many great benefits for those who add flax seeds to their diets because they can help reduce your risk of cancer, heart disease, arthritis, and it can also be a natural laxative. Flax seed is essential for a well balanced and healthy body and good mental health. Everyone should add flax seed supplements to their own diet.

There are many different forms of flax seed to choose from including raw flax seeds, flax seed oil, and flax seed supplements. Raw flax seeds offer the best nutrients because they haven't lost anything while being processed. Many people increase their consumption of flax seed by grinding it and then sprinkling it on muesli, soup, salad, and even various casseroles. They can also add a nutty flavour to baked goods such as muffins or pancakes. Keep in mind that as soon as you cook flax seed some of the nutritional value is destroyed and there are less essential Omega 3 fatty acids.

Flax seed oil is a great alternative for other types of oils that you often use for muesli. There are great recipes to make a delicious spreads or mayonnaise from it as well. You can consume one tablespoon of it by itself each day if you prefer. Capsules and liquid supplements are a common daily routine for many who want to add more essential Omega 3 fatty acids to their diet.

Before you add flax seeds to your diet, you need to be aware of a couple of issues. If you consume too much flax seed you can gain weight, but that is true of most anything. Flax seeds can go bad over time so don't buy too much at one time. Store them in a cool, dry, and dark location inside the refrigerator or freezer. After you have ground them you need to consume them within a few days. It is rare, but some people are allergic to flax seeds so if you have any type of reaction make sure you see a doctor immediately.

Understanding why you eat certain foods is essential in maintaining life long health habits. Certainly, pleasing taste and visual appeal is one reason we make food choices. Eating flax seeds may not seem to be appealing; however, choosing foods that keep our body working as a finely tuned machine is also the goal that healthy minded individuals try to achieve.

You Can Add Flaxseed in a Number of Different Ways

As whole seeds

You can put a handful of whole flaxseeds into pancake batter, bread dough, muffin dough and cookie mixtures. Scattering flaxseeds on the tops of these items just before baking them can also give an extra crunch and fuller flavour to the completed product. Baked goods with seeds on the top also look more interesting and tempting to people admiring them before eating.

Whole flaxseeds

As milled seeds

Flaxseed Meal

Milled flaxseed consists of flaxseed that has been ground up to make flour otherwise known as flaxseed meal. You can buy ready milled flaxseed from most supermarkets, health food shops and from the internet. You can also make your own milled flaxseed by putting it through your coffee grinder. This milled flaxseed has all of the nutrients of the whole seeds but they are easier for the body to access. As soon as flaxseed has been milled it starts to lose some of its nutrients and as a result it is better to mill your own and make it as you need it. Commercially milled flaxseed meal is sealed in air tight bags so that as much of the nutrients as possible are maintained. Once the packaging is opened or if you have any self milled flour it should be stored in the freezer or refrigerator. Milled flaxseed can be added to smoothies, cereal mixes, soups and baked foods. Here is a list of other foods that you might think about sprinkling with or mixing in milled flaxseed:

Peanut Butter and Jelly Sandwiches
Pancakes: simply sprinkle it into the batter.
French toast
Spaghetti
Meatballs
Meatloaf
Pizza
Bagels with cream cheese
Toast with butter and jelly
Tortilla and cream cheese
Yogurt and fruit
Cottage or ricotta cheese and fruit
Yogurt
Ricotta cheese
Peanut butter and cinnamon
Any nut butter
Cinnamon, sweetener, and butter
Chopped Nuts
Berries

Chopped Apple and cinnamon
Chopped Peaches
Sugar Free Maple Syrup
Other sugar free syrups
Sugar free jam
Unsweetened coconut milk
Butter
Shredded cheese
Shredded cheese and chilis
Pepper cheese
Cheese and chives
Cheese and garlic

As roasted seeds

You can easily make your own roasted flax seeds. Take a baking sheet and cover it with whole flaxseeds. You can pile the seeds up on the tray so that they are up to a half inch in depth. Put the baking sheet into an oven preheated to 180C and roast the flaxseeds for about 15 minutes making sure that you stir and mix them up a few times as they cook. Allow the roasted seeds to cool and then you can use them on such things as a topping for yoghurt or ice cream and sprinkled on salads. Roasted flaxseeds have a fantastic crunchy texture with a great nutty flavour. Once you have tried this you won't use sesame seeds on your salad again. Any remaining roasted flaxseeds can be stored in an airtight container.

Roasted Flaxseeds

Flaxseed as a Substitute

Substitute good fats for bad fats

You can replace any bad oils, animal fats or those low in omega 3 in a recipe by using ground flaxseed meal. The general rule is to use a 3 to 1 ratio. So, you should use 3 tablespoons of flaxseed meal to substitute for every 1 tablespoon of butter, cooking oil or margarine that you were previously using. You can use flaxseed meal instead of all of the existing fat or just part of it depending on what you are trying to achieve. You need to keep in mind that the milled flaxseed behaves slightly differently to normal fat in that it will tend to make foods brown at a faster rate when they are baked.

Another way to do this substitution is to use flaxseed oil itself. You can buy flaxseed oil from a shop or if you have a pressing machine, you can press your own oil directly from the seeds

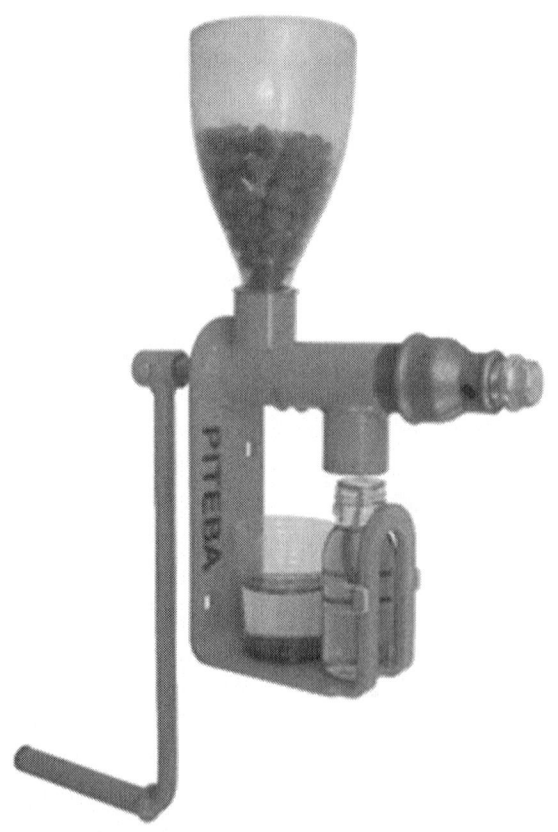

Oil Press to get oil out of flaxseeds

Again you should use a 3 to 1 ratio. As a result 1 cup of flaxseed oil can be used to substitute for a third of a cup of ordinary oil. Flaxseed oil tastes rather like butter and has only 20g of saturated fat and no cholesterol compared to ordinary butter which contains 117g of saturated fat and 488mg of cholesterol. This means that flaxseed oil is a far healthier option.

Flaxseed oil

Substitute flaxseed flour for processed flour

Processed flour is basically very nutrient poor. All the good stuff has been stripped away leaving the starch of the flour and very little else. This has been recognised for a long time and because of this extra vitamins and minerals are often added back into it. Flaxseed flour on the other hand contains lots of useful nutrients in addition to the omega 3 fatty acids indicated earlier. Flaxseed contains lots of vitamins and minerals as well as specific healthy substances such as lignans. It is no wonder that people want to add flaxseed to their diets whenever they can.

Due to the fat content of milled flaxseed you can't replace all of the processed flour in your recipe. This means that you are adding fat to any of the recipes that you decide to substitute milled flaxseed for normal flour. The good news is that you can use flaxseed meal to replace up to 15% of the normal flour in any recipe without having to go on to change the fat content of the recipe itself. The flaxseed meal will add to the flavour and nutrient content to any baked food that it is added to. Although flaxseed contains no gluten, when it is used at a 15% substitution it doesn't lead to a gluten free product. It does, however, reduce the gluten content which may be helpful in some situations. When using yeast as a rising agent with a milled flaxseed substitution it is a good idea to put an extra twenty five percent of yeast in the recipe.

Substitute flaxseed for wheat germ

Flaxseeds can be used in recipes as a substitute for wheat germ. Wheat germ is used in a number of cereals and breads. Wheat germ can be a real issue for people who have gluten intolerance. Substituting flax seeds can really help improve the lives of people with such problems. In addition to this the food will have a softer and chewier texture which is great for such delicacies as cookies.

Substitute flaxseed for chicken eggs

People who have an allergy to eggs or who are vegans can have real problems when it comes to producing a number of different baked foods. Eggs are a very important ingredient in a lot of recipes that require baking. There are a number of egg substitutes that can be bought in shops but they can be difficult to get and as well as this they can end up costing a lot of money for what they are. Flax seeds on the other hand are relatively cheap and readily available in most health food shops.

Eggs perform specific jobs in the recipes that they are used. The protein in eggs can help to build structure to the food. The protein in the egg forms a strong network when it is cooked. This is similar to the way that gluten works in wheat breads when they are baked. Egg protein can also form foam when it is whipped. This foam will trap air and is important when it comes to getting cakes to rise when they are baked. The trapped air expands when it is heated creating air bubbles in the cake which cause it to rise. Eggs can also act as an emulsifier. This means that they allow oils and water to mix. Normally they just separate out into layers with a layer of oil floating on the water. An emulsifier will make the oil spread through the food and water will tend to remain in the food longer making it moist. In turn this will give you soft textured foods that remain fresh for a lot longer. This emulsification is used in the making of ice creams, moist bouncy cakes and cookies that are chewy with a soft texture.

When it comes to looking for an egg substitute it needs to perform as many of the above functions as possible. Flaxseeds are one of the best things that you can use when you are trying to replace eggs in a recipe. Flax seeds have a layer of mucilage under the seed coat that results in a flax gel when it is released from the seed. The mucilage is made up of complex polysaccharides which tend to be long molecules that intertwine when added to water. Flax gel has many of the egg properties that we need for baking. For a start, the flax gel takes up and hangs onto water which is good for making the food moist and soft textured. The complex nature of the polysaccharide network means that it can also help in structure building. Flax gel also acts as a low foaming agent. These are the things that make flax gel a good egg substitute. Most other vegan egg substitutes can only achieve 2 of the egg function detailed above. As you can see flax gel can do all 3.

Despite all of these advantages flax seeds will never be exactly the same as eggs. They perform slightly differently and you need to take this into account when using them. Flax seeds aren't as good as eggs when used as a foaming agent. This means that foods that rely on air bubbles for their structure are more difficult or impossible to make. Very airy desserts such as choux pastry, angel food cake and popovers will not really work the same with flax gel. The structure mechanism in flax gel also works differently. It tends to stick the food components together rather than acting as a protein reinforcing network as eggs do when they are cooked in dough and batters. In the end you have to take into consideration the limitations of flax seeds when you make substitutions in different recipes.

The easiest way to substitute for eggs is to use milled flaxseed. You can buy ready milled flax seeds or mill your own using a coffee grinder or blender spice attachment. You can use a mixture of flaxseed meal and water as a substitute for eggs in a recipe. This is useful when used in pancakes, muffins and cookies if you have an allergy to eggs, don't want to use eggs or simply if you just don't have any eggs at a particular time. You should place one tablespoon of flaxseed meal in 3 tablespoons of hot water for each egg that is listed in the recipe. Mix well and let the mixture sit for a little while before using it. This doesn't work exactly the same as using eggs and can result in a chewier and denser product. This way of producing egg substitute, although being quick, can give rise to certain problems such as imparting a slight mealy flavour. This usually isn't a problem in a lot baked goods unless you use more than three tablespoons of flax meal in your recipe. In addition to this, the flaxseed meal may show up as golden grains in sauces, light coloured cakes and frostings. This is not the best method if you are trying to achieve an even light colour in your food.

Another, but more difficult way to use flaxseed is to boil the whole seeds in water and then strain off the gel from the seed coats which are then discarded. This then gets rid of the problems indicted in the previous paragraph when using flaxseed meal. When you use flaxseed gel in this way as an egg substitute it is best to mix it with the water based ingredients first. You can't whisk the flaxseed gel into the oil part of a recipe because the gel itself is water based and therefore won't mix with the oil. This is one way where eggs differ to the flax gel substitute. When flaxseed gel is used rather than flaxseed meal it works more like an actual egg as there are no ground particles in the gel. In addition to this the gel imparts much less flavour to the recipe and doesn't give a rough texture compared to flaxseed meal. This gel is quite pure and as a result you can easily add more of it to a recipe when you need a softer and chewier texture for example in the case of cookies and ice creams. The gel method is, however, more difficult to do and as a result if you don't bake very often it may end up being too much trouble to bother with.

Making Flaxseed Gel

The first stage is to put five tablespoons of flaxseed and three cups of water into a small saucepan. These measurements will result in about 1 cup of gel. Adjust the ingredient amounts depending on how much gel you require. Leave the pan uncovered and place on a medium to high heat. Bring the pan to the boil and then reduce until it is simmering. Stir the mixture every now and then to help release the gel. Continue to heat the pan until the mixture becomes thick and gelatinous. You should end up with a very thick gel as the gel is released from the seeds and some of the water is boiled off.

The next stage is to strain off the gel from the remains of the seed husks. To do this you need a sieve that has holes small enough to stop the seed husks passing through but large enough to allow the gel to pass as easily as possible. For this purpose you will find that a colander will work better than something like cheesecloth. You should start to strain the mixture as soon as the heating stage is completed. If you leave it to cool you will find that the gel will become too thick to pass through the holes in the colander. You can encourage the gel through the colander by using a spatula to scrape the gel over the mesh. Collect the gel in a bowl and when you have finished discard the husks of the seeds. If you can't sieve the mixture straight away you can reheat it later on so that the gel becomes thinner again. Put the collected gel into a small bowl and allow it to cool down to room temperature. This will probably take about an hour.

If you are not using the gel straight away you can store it in the refrigerator for about a week or in a freezer for about three months. When it comes to using the flax gel you will find that three tablespoons of the gel is about the same as one egg. When freezing the gel it is a good idea to separate the gel out into 3 tablespoon portions before freezing. This means that you already have the gel in one egg lots. This will make for quicker use when you need the gel in your recipes.

When it comes to measuring out the gel you may have problems. This is caused by the thickness of the gel and the fact that it tends to cling to itself. Measuring this out using tablespoons may be near impossible. As a result it is best to use a food grade syringe. With one of these you can easily suck up portions of the gel and then push it into the recipe ingredients where you need it. You should note that the syringe will be graduated in ml and that 45 ml is the same as 3 tablespoons of the gel or equivalent to 1 egg.

Low Carb Diets and Flaxseed

Low carb diets are diets designed to help people lose weight. The carb bit stands for 'carbohydrate'. We usually eat carbohydrate to give us energy for all the things we do from day to day. Carbohydrate is found in many of the staple foods across the world including potatoes, rice, wheat and cassava. The main carbohydrate in these is one called starch. The other main carbohydrate type includes all of the different types of sugars in food.

Starch in staple foods is responsible for feeding the majority of people across the world and is therefore very important. Starch is therefore a good food when it is taken in the correct amounts. It is unfortunate that many people in the Western world have such good supplies of cheap food that they over indulge and get fat and eventually obese. There is therefore a need to reduce the amount of food that people in the West eat. As a result there have been many, many diets that have been formulated to help people lose their excess weight.

Dieting should be simple: eat less food and do more exercise. However, as we all know the body has ways of making us eat the food while it is plentiful just in case we need it for times of starvation. Diets are supposed to make it easier for us to resist the urge to eat too much food and also help the body burn up all of the stored food.

One such regime is the low carb diet. During this kind of diet you replace carbohydrate foods with other foods such as fats and protein which provide us with the energy that we require. Fats and protein are also supposed to help suppress cravings for food as well as making the body work harder and so burn up stored fat.

The 'Atkins' diet is one well known version of a low carb diet. Flaxseeds are an ideal food to be part of a low carb diet. The reason for this is that they have virtually no carbohydrate in them and a lot of oil. Not only this, but, the oil itself is the good omega 3 healthy stuff. A number of the recipes given in the 'Recipes' section below are designed to be low carbohydrate and as a result are ideal for people on a low carb diet.

Help with Coeliac Disease

Coeliac disease is an autoimmune condition which is related to the grains such as wheat barley and rye. It is actually the gluten in these grains that is responsible for the condition. The gluten causes an immune reaction in people with coeliac disease. During this reaction the lining of the small intestine gets damaged. In addition to this there are other parts of the body that may get affected. The symptoms that people show vary between individuals and can be at different severity levels. It is believed that 1 in a 100 people may suffer from some degree of coeliac disease. However, not all of these will get a diagnosis or seek one. There can also be confusion with other conditions such as wheat intolerance and irritable bowel syndrome. Here are some of the main symptoms shown by individuals with the condition:

Diarrhoea,
Excessive Flatulence
Constipation
Feelings of nausea and vomiting
Stomach pain
Stomach cramps
Bloating
Iron and vitamin B deficiency
Tiredness
Headaches

Weight loss
Mouth ulcers
Alopecia
Skin rashes
Tooth enamel problems
Osteoporosis
Depression
Infertility
Miscarriages
Joint pain
Bone pain
Neurological problems

If you find that these symptoms can be tied down to the times when you eat food containing gluten you should consult your doctor in order to get a diagnosis. Obviously people may suffer symptoms such as those above due to other medical conditions. You need a doctor to diagnose coeliac disease before you start worrying about it.

One of the difficulties for people suffering from coeliac disease is the ability to avoid foods that contain gluten. This is especially the case when it comes to such things as supermarket ready meals where the list of things added to the food maybe long and varied. Some products are obvious ones, such as bread. This contains wheat and gluten is in the flour used to make the bread. Others aren't so obvious, such as beer. The beer is made from barley and some gluten enters the beer while it is being made. Even if you can avoid the products with gluten in them there is then the problem of what to replace it with. Flours have to be selected that don't contain gluten. This can be done but there are usually only a small number of such products available from shops such as supermarkets. They may also be expensive. Flaxseeds don't contain gluten and as a result can be used to help replace some of the gluten containing ingredients in recipes. The recipes below in the 'Recipes' section contain details of how to use flaxseed flour to make some useful gluten free foods.

Flaxseeds can also be used in recipes to help people that have intolerance to wheat, and basically those recipes that are gluten free should also work with this condition. However, you should make sure that any of the additions to the recipe such as soy sauce don't contain any allergens that you might be sensitive to. If in doubt seek help from a medical professional.

Flaxseed Recipes

Getting the Main Ingredients

It is best to get the unrefined versions so that you are sure that you are getting the maximum amounts of omega 3 and other healthy substances:

Whole Golden Flaxseeds
Flaxseed Meal
Flaxseed oil

You should be able to get these from health food shops and possible some supermarkets. Alternatively you can get them on the internet by way of Amazon.com

Banana Flax Bread

Ingredients

1 cup sugar
2 eggs
1 tsp vanilla
1/2 cup butter
1/3 cup milk
4 mashed bananas
1 1/3 cup plain flour
1/3 cup flaxseed meal
1 tsp baking soda
1/4 tsp baking powder
1/2 tsp salt

Method

Mash the bananas

Mix together the sugar, eggs, vanilla, butter and milk in a large bowl. Once this is well mixed add the mashed bananas followed by the plain flour, ground flaxseed, baking soda, baking powder and salt. Mix all of the ingredients well.

Bake the bread as small loaves by putting the dough into pans 4 inches by 6 inches or using mini pans. Put the baking pans into a preheated oven set to 180C for about 45 minutes.

Children will love this bread especially when it comes straight out of the oven.

Oatmeal Bran and Flax Meal Muffins

Ingredients

1 1/2 cups general purpose white flour
3/4 cup flaxseed meal
3/4 cup oat bran
1 cup brown sugar
2 tsp baking soda
1 tsp baking powder
1/2 tsp salt
2 tsp cinnamon
1 1/2 cups shredded carrots
2 apples
1/2 cup raisins
1 cup chopped nuts
3/4 cup milk
2 eggs
1 tsp vanilla

Method

Peel and shred the apples.

Beat the eggs

In a large bowl mix all of the dry ingredients together. Make sure that they are well combines. Stir in the carrots, apples, raisins and chopped nuts.

In another bowl mix together the milk, beaten eggs, and vanilla. Pour these wet ingredients into the large bowl containing the dry ingredients. Stir everything together until all of the dry ingredients are moistened. Make sure that you don't over mix everything.

Put the batter into muffin cups so that they are three quarters filed. This recipe should make around fifteen muffins. Bake the muffins in a preheated oven set to 180C for around 20 minutes or until they are nicely browned on the tops.

Cheesy Flaxseed Breaded Chicken Breast

Ingredients

1 tbsp flaxseed meal
5 tbsp water

1 Pound boneless chicken breast
1 cup plain bread crumbs
1/4 cup grated parmesan cheese
1 tsp dried basil
1 tsp dried oregano
1 tbsp garlic powder
3 tbsp flaxseed meal
1/2 cup frying oil

1 1/2 cups tomato sauce

Parmesan cheese
Fresh basil leaves

Method

Trim the chicken breast and rinse it in cold water.

Use 1 tbsp of flaxseed meal and 5 tbsp of water to make an egg wash substitute. Use a fork to mix it well.

Make a breading mixture by putting the bread crumbs, garlic, basil, oregano, flaxseed meal and parmesan cheese into a bowl and mixing everything together until it is well combined.

Heat up the tomato sauce in a small pan until it is hot.

Put the frying oil into a large frying pan and put it onto a medium to high heat.

Take the chicken breast and dip it into the egg substitute and then cover it well with the breading mixture. Add the chicken breast pieces gently one at a time to the frying oil in the hot pan. Fry the chicken for around 5 minutes until the coating becomes golden brown. Turn the chicken pieces over and fry the other side for about another 5 minutes until this too is a golden brown. Once the chicken is cooked through take the pan away from the heat. Place the cooked chicken on paper towel to help soak up the excess oil.

To serve the chicken put it on plates and cover with the tomato sauce. Garnish the plates with grated parmesan and fresh basil leaves.

Flaxseed Low Carb and Gluten Free Bread

Ingredients

2 cups flax seed meal
2 tsp mixed dried Italian herbs
1-2 tbsp Parmesan cheese
1 tbsp baking powder
1 tsp salt
Artificial sweetener same as 1 tbsp sugar
5 beaten eggs
1/2 cup water
1/3 cup extra virgin olive oil

Method

Put the flax seed meal, baking powder, herbs, Parmesan cheese, salt and sweetener into a large bowl and combine them well using a whisk.

Beat the eggs in another bowl and then mix in the olive oil and water.

Add the wet ingredients to the dry ingredients in the large bowl and combine them well. Let the mixture stand for a couple of minutes before pouring it into the centre of a well greased 10 inch by 15 inch baking pan. Use greased parchment paper on the base of the pan if sticking in the pan becomes an issue. Spread out the batter to get an even depth in the pan but keep it and inch or so away from the pan sides so that the layer isn't too thin.

Put the pan into a preheated oven set to 180C and bake for about 20 minutes until the top of the bread is browning and it springs back when the top is touched.

Leave the bread to cool and cut into slices ready to eat.

Flaxseed Low Carb and Gluten Free Pizza Base

Ingredients

1 1/2 cups flax seed meal
2 tsp baking powder
1 tsp salt
2 teaspoon dried Italian mixed herbs
Freshly ground black pepper
3 tbsp extra virgin olive oil
3 eggs
1/2 cup water

Method

Put the flax seed meal, baking powder, salt, herbs and pepper to taste into a large bowl and combine the ingredients together well.

Put the olive oil, eggs and water in another bowl and whisk them together. Add these wet ingredients to the dry ingredients in the large bowl and mix everything together until they are well combined.

Let the mixture stand for a few minutes until it has thickened a little. Pour the batter onto a well greased baking sheet and spread it out using a spatula until you have a pizza base that is about 12 inches round.

Put the baking tray into a preheated oven set to 180C and cook for about 15 minutes.

Add the toppings that you want to use and continue cooking until the pizza is cooked to your liking.

If you find the pizza base a little bland you can try adding any or all of the following: extra herbs, parmesan cheese and non sugar sweetener.

This pizza base will not have exactly the same consistency or crispness as you would get with a wheat flour one but with a little experimentation with cooking times you should be able to get something that is acceptable.

Strawberry and Flaxseed Smoothie

Ingredients

2 tbsp flax seeds
1 cup vanilla flavored soya milk
1 tsp lemon juice
1 cup strawberries
1 banana
6 tsp sugar

Method

Roughly chop the strawberries and the banana.

Place the soya milk, lemon juice, flax seeds, banana and sugar into a blender and whizz it all up until it is smooth and frothy.

Pour the smoothie into 2 glasses and serve.

Granola with Flaxseed

Ingredients

2 tsp ground cinnamon
1/2 tsp ground ginger
1/4 tsp salt
3 tbsp honey
2 tbsp extra virgin olive oil
2 tbsp maple syrup
2 tbsp water
1 tsp vanilla
2 cups whole oats
1/2 cup chopped pecan nuts
1/2 cup crisped rice cereal
1/4 cup milled flax seed

Method

Put the cinnamon, ginger, salt, honey, olive oil, maple syrup, vanilla and water into a large bowl and whisk them together. Add the oats, rice cereal, pecans and milled flax seeds and gently stir so combine.

Spread out the mixture on a parchment lined baking sheet. Put the baking sheet into a preheated oven set to 150C and bake until the granola is crisp and dry but not browned. This should take around 30 minutes. Allow the granola to cool before serving.

Cinnamon Muffins

Ingredients

1 1/2 cups whole wheat flour
1 1/2 cups milled flax seed
3/4 cup brown sugar
1 tbsp baking powder
3/4 tsp ground nutmeg
1 1/2 tsp ground cinnamon
2 cups milk
1 egg

Method

Mix the flour, flax seed, brown sugar, baking powder, nutmeg and cinnamon in a large bowl.

In a separate smaller bowl beat the egg and then add the milk and stir to combine.

Add the wet ingredients to the dry ingredients in the large bowl. Stir until the dry ingredients are moistened.

Use non stick muffin pans and fill the tins so that they are three quarters filled. Place the muffin tins into a preheated oven set to 180C. Cook the muffins for about 30 minutes or until they are light brown on the top. Once they are cooked place the muffins on cooling racks. Serve when cool.

Apple Pecan Muffins

Ingredients

1 1/4 cup flax seed meal
2 tsp baking powder
1 tbsp ground cinnamon
1 tsp nutmeg
1/2 tsp salt
3/4 cup sugar or equivalent artificial sweetener
4 large eggs, beaten
1/4 cup coconut oil
1/2 cup water
1 tbsp vanilla
1 medium apple
1/2 cup chopped pecan nuts

Method

Chop the apple into quite fine pieces.
Put the flaxseed meal, baking powder, cinnamon, nutmeg, salt, sugar, apple and pecans into a large mixing bowl. Combine everything well.
In a separate bowl beat the eggs and then add the coconut oil, water and vanilla. Whisk again to mix. Add these wet ingredients to the dry ingredients and mix them together until the dry ingredients are moist.

Allow the mixture to sit for about ten minutes and then put into well greased muffin pans. Put the muffin pans into a preheated oven set to 180C. Bake the muffins for about 20 minutes until a baking test skewer comes out clean and the mixture is cooked.

Use artificial sweetener if you are aiming to produce a low carbohydrate version.

Low Carb Blueberry and Walnut Muffins

Ingredients

1 cup whole fresh blueberries
1 1/4 cup flax seed meal
1 tsp baking powder
3 tbsp cinnamon
1 tsp nutmeg
1/2 tsp salt
4 large eggs, beaten
1/4 cup extra virgin olive oil
1/2 cup sugar free syrup
1 tbsp vanilla
2 tbsp grated orange peel
3/4 cup chopped walnuts

Method

Put the flax seed meal, baking powder, cinnamon, nutmeg and salt into a large bowl and mix until everything is combined well.

In another bowl beat the eggs and then stir in the olive oil, syrup and vanilla. Add these wet ingredients to the dry ingredients in the large bowl and mix until the dry ones are moistened.

Allow the batter to sit for about 10 minutes and then fold in the orange peel and blueberries.

Half fill greased muffin pans with the batter and then sprinkle with the chopped walnuts. This should make about 12 to 24 muffins depending on the size of your pans.

Put the muffin pans into a preheated oven set to 180C and bake for about 15 minutes. Use a testing skewer and remove from the oven once it comes out clean when inserted to the centre of the muffin.

Low Carb Duffins

Ingredients

1 cup flaxseed meal
1 cup almond meal
1 tbsp baking powder
1/4 tsp salt
1 1/4 tsp nutmeg
1 tsp cinnamon
1 cup artificial liquid sweetener
1/2 cup melted butter
4 eggs
1/2 cup plus 2 tbsp water

Duffin topping

1/2 cup powdered artificial sweetener
2 tsp cinnamon
2 tbsp melted butter

Method

Put the flaxseed meal, almond meal, baking powder, salt, nutmeg and cinnamon into a large bowl and mix together until the ingredients are well combined.

In another bowl beat the eggs and then mix in the liquid sweetener, melted butter and the water. Add these to the dry ingredients in the large bowl and mix them together well.

Put the mixture into well greased muffin pans making sure that they are each filled just over half way. It should make about 12 muffins. Put the muffin pans into a preheated oven set to 180C for about 20 minutes or until the tops are a golden brown and a testing skewer placed in the centre comes out clean. Remove the muffins from the oven.

Mix the sweetener and cinnamon for the topping and melt the butter. Once the muffins have cooled sufficiently take them from the pans and apply the toppings by first dipping in melted butter followed by the cinnamon sweetener topping.

Low Carb Cheesy Crackers

Ingredients

1 cup flaxseed meal
1/3 cup grated Parmesan cheese
1 tsp garlic powder
1/2 tsp cayenne pepper
1/2 teaspoon seasoned salt
3/4 cup water

Method

Put the flaxseed meal, parmesan, cayenne pepper, garlic powder, salt and water into a large bowl and mix them well.

Cover a baking sheet with foil and then spoon on the mixture from the bowl. Spread out the mixture with a wooden spatula so that it is an even thickness of about 3 to 4 mm.

Place the baking sheet into a preheated oven set to 200C for about 20 minutes. After this time turn off the heat but leave them in the oven for an hour to crisp up. Once it is cooked remove it from the oven and leave it to cool down to room temperature.

The cracker should become nice and crisp and you should then be able to peel it off the foil and break it up into pieces and serve on its own or with dips and spreads as a snack.

Low Carb Breakfast Cereal

Ingredients

1/4 cup flaxseed meal
1/2 tsp cinnamon
1/2 scoop vanilla protein powder
2 tbsp chunky peanut butter
1/3 cup boiling water
1 tbsp sugar free syrup

Method

Put the flaxseed meal, protein powder, and cinnamon into a breakfast bowl and stir to mix them together.

Spoon the peanut butter on top.

Pour on the boiling water and stir until it is combined well.

Let the mixture stand for a minute before stirring in the syrup. Eat while hot.

This low carb breakfast cereal is quick and easy to make. It contains a lot of fiber so consider working up to a full portion each day. If you eat this for breakfast it should keep you full until lunch. You can try changing the flavour of the protein powder for variation. Chocolate flavour protein is worth trying. It can all seem to have a slimy texture but the protein powder and peanut butter should help with this. If you find the texture difficult try changing the proportions of these in the recipe.

Low Carb Breakfast Smoothie

Ingredients

1 cup cold coffee
1 scoop low carb vanilla protein powder
1/2 cup coconut milk
2 tbsp flaxseed meal
Sweetener to taste
3-4 ice cubes

Method

Put all of the ingredients into a blender and whiz it up until you have the right consistency for you.

The longer you leave the smoothie to stand the thicker it will become due to the action of the gel released from the flaxseed meal.

Try chocolate flavoured protein powder for variation.

This smoothie will easily work as a breakfast replacement and keep you going until lunch.

Almond and Flaxseed Gluten Free Bread

Ingredients

1 1/2 cups almond flour
3/4 cup corn flour
1/4 cup flaxseed meal
1/2 tsp salt
1/2 tsp baking soda
4 eggs
1 tsp honey
1 tsp apple cider vinegar

Method

Put the almond flour, corn flour, flaxseed meal, salt and baking soda into a large bowl. Whisk them together to combine them.

In another bowl beat the eggs until they are frothy. Mix in the honey and the vinegar until everything is combined. Add the wet ingredients to the dry in the large bowl and mix them together until the dry ingredients are all moistened.

Pour the mixture into a 7 1/5 inch by 3 1/2 inch greased bread pan and then place in a preheated oven set to 180C. Bake the bread for about 30 minutes and then use a test skewer to make sure the bread is cooked in the middle. The skewer should come out clean, but if it doesn't cook it further until the skewer does come out clean.

Cool the cooked bread on a wire rack and serve when it reaches room temperature.

Flaxseed and Cashew Nut Energy Bar

Ingredients

2 cups cashew nuts
1/2 cup flaxseed meal
1/2 cup shredded coconut
1/2 cup cashew nut butter
1/2 tsp salt
1/2 cup coconut oil
4 drops stevia
1 tbsp honey
1 tbsp vanilla extract
1 cup dark chocolate chunks

Method

Put the cashew nuts, flaxseed meal, coconut, cashew butter and salt into a food processor and give it a short pulse for a few seconds

Put the coconut oil into a small pan and melt it slowly on a low heat. Take the pan away from the heat and mix in the stevia, honey and vanilla. Add this mixture to the contents of the food processor and pulse the mixture until you get a course paste.

Put the mixture into a baking dish about eight inches square and use a spatula to spread it out evenly.

Harden the contents of the dish by putting it in the refrigerator for about an hour.

Melt the chocolate chunks in a small pan by stirring it over a low heat. Remove the mixture dish from the refrigerator and spread the chocolate on the top. Put the dish back into the refrigerator for another hour so that the chocolate becomes hard as well.

Remove the dish from the refrigerator and cut into bar sizes.

Quick and Easy Cookies

Ingredients

14 digestive biscuits
1/2 cup muesli
2 tbsp wheat bran
1 tbsp flaxseeds meal
1/2 cup peanut butter
2 drops of vanilla essence
2 tbsp chocolate chips
Desiccated coconut

Method

Break the digestive biscuits up into pieces and put into a mixing bowl. Use your hands or the back of a spoon to break the biscuits up into a chunky powder.

Stir in the wheat bran, flaxseed meal, muesli, peanut butter, vanilla, and chocolate chips. Mix until everything is combined well.

Knead the mixture in order to make dough. Separate the dough into 12 equal parts and then roll each one into a ball. Flatten each ball with your hand or a rolling pin so that you have 12 thick discs.

Put the coconut into a shallow bowl and then dredge the discs through it so that both sides become coated with the coconut.

You can serve these cookies straight away or save until later by putting them into a biscuit box or other suitable container.

Vegetable and Flaxseed Fritters

Ingredients

1 small courgette
1/2 tsp salt
1/2 cup flax seed meal
2 tbsp coconut flour
2 tsp dried oregano
1 tsp ground marjoram
3/4 tsp freshly ground black pepper
1/2 tsp sea salt
1 cup crumbled feta
1/4 cup shopped green onions
2 large eggs
6 tbsp extra virgin olive oil
1/4 cup Greek style yogurt

Method

Finely shred the courgette until you have about 2 cups. Put these in a sieve, sprinkle with salt and leave for about an hour to drain.

Put the coconut flour, flaxseed meal, oregano, marjoram, black pepper and sea salt into a large bowl and mix together until everything is well combined.

Mix in the feta cheese, green onions, shredded courgette and eggs. Make sure that everything is well mixed together. Shape the mixture into patties that are about 3/4 inch thick.

Put the oil into a large deep frying pan and put on a medium heat. Once the oil is hot place the fritters into the pan and cook them until they are nice and brown on both sides. Put the cooked fritters onto paper towels to drain and continue cooking until all of the fritters are done. Serve while nice and warm with a garnish of Greek yoghurt.

Quick and Easy Low Carb Flaxseed Wraps

Ingredients

2 tbsp flaxseed meal
1 egg
1/4 tsp baking powder
Non-stick cooking oil spray

Method

Take a dinner plate and spray on the non-stick cooking oil spray so that the cooked wrap can easily be removed.

Put the egg, flaxseed meal and baking powder onto the plate and mix the ingredients together so that they are well combined.

Set the microwave between sixty and ninety seconds depending on your specific microwave. You may need to find the best setting by experimentation. Put the plate and mixed ingredients into the microwave and let it cook. Once it is cooked remove from the microwave and ease off the wrap using a plastic spatula.

Fill your cooked wrap with the ingredients that you want to use and roll it up ready to eat. These wraps are ideal for breakfast with such things as fried eggs and ham or simply honey.

Flaxseed Bread Made in a Bread Machine

Ingredients

1 1/3 cups water
2 tbsp softened butter
3 tbsp honey
11/2 cups plain bread flour
11/3 cups whole wheat flour
1 tsp salt
1 tsp active dry yeast
1/2 cup ground flaxseed meal

Method

This is a very easy bread to make. Collect all of the ingredients together and then put them in the bread machine pan starting with the water.

Set the bread machine to bake a basic white loaf and then press start. This will probably take somewhere in the region of 3 hours.

This will produce a very light loaf that will work the same as normal bread. You can add things such as sunflower seeds, raisins or olives to make variations on this bread. Add these extra ingredients when the warning sound goes off during the kneading part of the machine cycle.

Flaxseed and Wholemeal Flour Pancakes

Ingredients

1 cup of wholemeal flour
2 tsp flaxseed meal
1 cup skimmed milk
1 egg
1 tsp honey

Method

Put the whole meal flour and the flaxseed meal into a mixing bowl and then mix it up with a whisk.

Add the skimmed milk and once again use the whisk to combine it with the flour.

Crack the egg into a small bowl and use the whisk to break it up and mix the yolk with the white. Add the egg to the dry ingredients and use the whisk to mix everything together.

Mix until you have a thick batter and then leave it to stand for a while. Mix in the honey. Use more than 1 tsp if you want to.

Spray a small frying pan with spray olive oil. Put the pan onto a medium heat. Once the oil is moving around and is hot put some of the batter into the pan. The batter should make about 6 pancakes so divide it up accordingly.

Gently tip the pan so that the mixture fills the bottom of the pan and the oil circulates around. Cook for about 1 and half minutes and then turn the pancake and cook the other side.

Once the pancake is cooked slide it onto a plate and eat with honey and lemon or add your favourite topping.

Flaxseed Raita

Ingredients

1 medium cucumber
2 tbsp roasted flaxseeds
1/2 cup yoghurt
1/4 tsp roasted cumin powder
Salt
Pinch red chilli powder
1 tbsp chopped fresh coriander

Method

Peel the cucumber.

Grate the cucumber and collect in a mixing bowl.

Whisk the yoghurt and then add it to the cucumber. Next add the cumin powder, chilli, coriander and salt to taste. Mix the ingredients so that everything is combined.

Put the mixture into the refrigerator to cool.

Put the mixture into small serving bowls and sprinkle with the roasted flax seed when you are ready to serve.

Fig and Flaxseed Biscuits

Ingredients

1 cup wholemeal flour
1 cup flaxseed meal
1 tsp ground cinnamon
1 1/2 cups figs
2 eggs
1/3 cup soft brown sugar
1/2 cup almonds

Method

Put the flaxseed and almonds into a food processor and start to chop while slowly adding the figs until everything is chopped up. Add the cinnamon, eggs and brown sugar and process until everything is mixed.

Spread the mixture out onto a parchment lined baking sheet and then put into a preheated oven set to 220C. Bake the biscuits for about 18 minutes. Remove form the oven and leave to cool. And then cut into suitable sized squares.

Low Carb Flaxseed Crisp Thins

Ingredients

1 cup flaxseed meal
1 tsp stevia
1 tsp garlic powder
1 tsp onion powder
1/2 cup water
Freshly ground black pepper

Method

Put the flaxseed meal into a mixing bowl and then add the stevia, garlic powder and onion powder. Mix the ingredients well to combine them. Add in the water and continue to stir. Make sure that all of the dry ingredients have been evenly moistened and then leave the mixture to stand a while so that the water starts to get absorbed. Stir the mixture again to get an even texture.

Roll the mixture up into small balls and place them on a baking sheet covered with parchment paper. Leave gaps between each ball of mixture. Cut a small square of parchment paper about 3 or 4 inches square. And place it over one of mixture balls. Take a flat solid object such as a flat spoon or the bottom of a jar and press down on the parchment paper squashing the mixture flat. Get the disc produced as thin as you can without it breaking up. Repeat squashing all of the mixture balls flat. You may need to experiment with the size of mixture balls that you use and the space between them. The larger the ball the bigger the flat disc that is produced. Once you have flattened all of the mixture balls put fresh ground black pepper on the top of each one according to taste

Put the baking tray into a preheated oven set to 200C and cook for about 8 minutes. Turn off the oven after this time but leave the crisp thins in the oven to crisp up. Serve with a suitable cream or cream cheese dip.

Instead of black pepper you can try covering the tops of the crisp thins with dried herbs such as rosemary, basil, oregano, chilli powder etc. You can try producing a tray of crisp thins that all have different toppings according to what you like

Flaxseed Waffles

Ingredients

1 cup plain flour
1/2 cup whole wheat flour
1/4 cup flax seed meal
1 tbsp baking powder
1/2 tsp salt
2 cups milk
1/3 cup extra virgin olive oil
2 eggs

Method

Put the plain flour, whole wheat flour, flaxseed flour, baking powder and salt into a large bowl and mix until everything is well combined.

In another bowl lightly beat the eggs and then add the milk and olive oil and stir to mix. Add these wet ingredients to the dry ingredients and mix to blend them in.

Pour about three quarters of a cup of the batter onto the surface of a preheated waffle and cook until they are how you like your waffles.

Remove from the waffle iron and add toppings.

Vegan Flaxseed and Nut Meat Loaf

Ingredients

1 tbsp extra virgin olive oil
1 medium onion
1 rib of celery
4 cloves of garlic
1 pound of mushrooms
1/2 cup vegetable broth
1 1/2 cup pecan nuts
1 1/2 cup walnuts
1 1/2 cups cooked rice
1 cup oats
2 tbsp soy sauce
1 tsp dried parsley
1 tsp poultry seasoning
3/4 cup water
4 tbsp flaxseed meal
Salt and pepper to taste

Method

Dice the onion, celery and mushrooms.

Mince the garlic.

Put the olive oil into a large frying pan and put it on a medium to high heat setting. Add the onions and celery and cook until the onions become translucent.

Put the garlic, vegetable broth and mushrooms into the frying pan and stir together with the onions and celery. Once the mixture is simmering continue cooking until the majority of the water is absorbed.

Put the pecans and walnuts into a food processor and chop them up finely. Put the cooked rice, oats, parsley, poultry seasoning, soy sauce, pepper and salt into a large mixing bowl and add the chopped nuts. Stir the ingredients to combine them and then add the contents of the frying pan. Continue to stir until everything is well combined.

Put the flaxseed meal into a small bowl and mix in the water. Continue to mix until it becomes thickened. Add this to the ingredients in the large mixing bowl and stir until everything is combined well.
.
Put a parchment lining into a nine inch baking pan and then add the meatloaf mixture. Use a spatula to spread it out evenly in the pan.

Put the pan into a preheated oven set to 190C and bake for about 60 minutes until it is browned on the top. Use a testing skewer to make sure it is cooked in the centre.

Once the meat loaf is cooked remove it from the oven and place on a cooling rack for about 30 minutes. Remove the meat loaf from the pan with the help of a knife and put it on a plate ready to serve.

Flaxseed and Almond Burgers

Ingredients

2 cloves garlic
1 cup raw almonds
1/2 cup flaxseed meal
2 tbsp balsamic vinegar
2 tbsp coconut oil
Sea salt to taste

Method

This is a raw food recipe and as a result requires no cooking.

The ingredients listed will make 2 burgers.

Put all of the ingredients into a food processor and process until all the ingredients are chopped and well combined. You may need the pulse feature to make sure all of the nuts are actually chopped.

Remove the mixture from the food processor and make into 2 patties. These burgers are very filling and only need to be served with a side salad. You can serve these right away with salad and salad dressings or you can heat them up a little in an oven set to no more that 180C. You may want to reduce the amount of garlic if you don't want it lingering on your breath for too long.

Flaxseed and Hot Pepper Smoothie

Ingredients

1 banana
1 mango, peeled and pit removed
1 lime
1/2 jalapeno pepper
1.5 cups water
1 cup ice
1 tbsp flaxseed meal
1 tbsp protein powder
1 tbsp honey
1 tbsp hemp oil

Method

Peel and chop the banana and put into a blender.

Peel the mango, remove the seed, cut into slices and put into the blender.

Juice the lime and add the juice to the blender.

Add the jalapeno pepper, water, ice, flaxseed meal, protein, honey and hemp oil. Whiz the whole thing up and serve in 2 glasses.

Flaxseed and Chilli Corn Bread

Ingredients

1 cup yellow cornmeal
3/4 cup whole wheat flour
1/4 cup flaxseed meal
2 tsp baking powder
1/2 tsp baking soda
3/4 tsp salt
1/2 tsp black pepper
4 green onions
3/4 cup grated Parmesan cheese
1 medium Serrano pepper
1/2 cup frozen yellow corn
3/4 cup milk
1 cup buttermilk
1 large egg
2 tsp honey
3 tbsp canola oil

Method

Defrost the corn.

Finely chop the green onions.

Remove the seeds from the Serrano pepper and then mince it.

Put the cornmeal, whole wheat flour, flaxseed meal, baking soda, baking powder, pepper and salt into a large mixing bowl and whisk it together until it is well combined. Whisk in the green onions, Parmesan, Serrano pepper and the corn.

Put the milk, buttermilk, egg, honey and canola oil into another bowl and whisk to combine them. Add these ingredients to the dry ingredients in the large mixing bowl and stir everything until everything is just combined. Make sure that you don't mix it too much.

Pour the batter into a thirteen by nine inch baking pan and then put it into a preheated oven set to 200C. Bake the bread for about 20 minutes. The bread is cooked when the top has browned to a golden colour and a testing skewer put to the centre of the bread comes out clean.

This bread is dense and full of flavour. It is ideal to be served as part of a Southern style breakfast or meal of green beans.

Flaxseed Savoury Slice

Ingredients

100g Flaxseed meal
300g wholemeal flour
4 carrots
2 eggs
1/4 tsp ground nutmeg
2 tsp ground cinnamon

Method

Grate the carrots

Put the flaxseed meal into a large mixing bowl and then add the ground cinnamon, nutmeg and wholemeal flour and mix with a whisk to combine.

Put the carrot and the dry contents of the mixing bowl into a food processor and then add the eggs. Whiz it up in the processor until it is well combined.

Take the mixture from the processor bowl and put it on a baking sheet and spread it out using a spatula until it is about 1/2 inch thick.

Put the baking sheet in a preheated oven set to 200C for about 20 minutes. Once it is cooked remove it from the oven and allow it to cool. Once it is cooled cut into suitably sized squares.

Flaxseed and Greek Yoghurt

Ingredients

4 tbsp Greek yoghurt
1tsp Cocoa powder
1 tbsp pecan nuts
2 tbsp flaxseeds
1 tsp Maple syrup

Method

This is a layered dish that can be produced very quickly and is based on a traditional Greek recipe.

Take a desert bowl and put 2 tablespoons of yoghurt in the bottom. Put about 1/2 teaspoon of cocoa powder on top of this followed by 1/2 a tablespoon of pecan nuts and then a tablespoon of flaxseed.

For the next layer put another 2 tablespoons of Greek yoghurt and once again 1/2 teaspoon cocoa powder on top of this followed by 1/2 a tablespoon of pecan nuts and then a tablespoon of flaxseed. On top of this put about a teaspoon of maple syrup.

Eat this yoghurt dish straight away. You can have it for breakfast as a dessert or simply as a snack.

Flaxseed Tea

Ingredients

4 tbsp flaxseed meal
2 cups boiling water
Pinch or 2 of ground cinnamon
Honey

Method

Put the flaxseed meal into a large heat proof measuring jug. Add the 2 cups of boiling water and steep the tea for around 10 minutes.

After the 10 minutes, pour the tea through a strainer, with a fine mesh, into another suitably sized container.

Add a couple of pinches of ground cinnamon and then sweeten to your own taste with honey or syrup. Transfer the tea to one large mug or 2 smaller tea cups.

Flaxseed and Whole Grain Rice

Ingredients

1 1/4 cups short grain brown rice
1/4 cup wild rice
1/4 cup lentils
1/4 cup quinoa
3 tablespoons flaxseed meal
4 cups warm water

Method

Put the brown rice, wild rice, quinoa, lentils and flaxseed meal into a large pan. Mix to combine the different grains.

Add the water and leave to sit at room temperature for between 1 and 4 hours depending on the time that you have got. During this time the grains will take up the water.

Put a lid on the pan and put it on a high heat. Once the pan is boiling reduce the heat so that it simmers nice and gently. Cook the rice for about 45 minutes or until just about all of the liquid has been absorbed or been driven off.

Remove the pan from the heat and leave to stand for half an hour with the lid on. After this time remove the lid and let it cool back down to room temperature.

This rice should be served at room temperature and is especially good with sushi and salads.

Flaxseed Oil Salad Dressing

Ingredients

3 tbsp apple cider vinegar
1 tbsp freshly chopped chives
1 tbsp freshly chopped parsley
1/2 tsp dried basil
1/2 tsp dried oregano
1/2 tsp dry mustard
1 large clove garlic
3 tbsp flaxseed oil
Dash of cayenne
Salt
Freshly ground black pepper

Method

Roughly chop the garlic

Put the apple cider vinegar, chives, parsley, oregano, basil garlic and mustard into a blender and blend the mixture until it is nice and smooth.

Slowly add the flaxseed oil and continue to blend until you have a mixture that is just about becoming creamy.

Add the cayenne and season to taste with salt and pepper.

Use the dressing by drizzling it over salads or steamed vegetables.

Flaxseed Muesli

Ingredients

2 cups rolled oats
2/3 cup rye flakes
1/3 cup coarsely chopped almonds
2 tbsp flaked coconut
1/2 cup raisins
2 tbsp honey
1/2 tsp vanilla extract
Pinch of cinnamon
1/4 cup flaxseed meal
Olive oil cooking spray

Method

Use the cooking oil spray to cover a baking sheet. Put the oats and rye flakes onto the baking sheet and spread them out to make a thin layer.

Put the baking sheet into a preheated oven set to 180C and bake for about 10 minutes.

Stir in the almonds and coconut and then bake for a further 10 minutes.

Turn off the oven and then stir in the raisins.

Put the honey into a small bowl and heat in the microwave for about 10 seconds. Remove from the microwave and stir in the vanilla and cinnamon. Pour this mixture over the muesli on the baking tray and stir the mixture so that everything is coated.

Put the baking tray with the coated muesli back into the now turned off oven and leave there for about 2 hours until it has returned to room temperature.

Put the muesli into a bowl and then stir in the flaxseed meal.

Serve the muesli for breakfast with yoghurt or milk.

Conclusion

Fields of flax

This book should have given you a lot of ideas about how to include flaxseeds in your diet. There are a number of reasons for using flaxseeds in meals besides the simple one that they provide fantastic nutrition in the form of healthy omega 3 fatty acids and other interesting healthy elements. Other reasons for using flax include the fact that it doesn't contain gluten and that it can be made into a very good egg substitute. The 36 recipes given here should give you a head start when it comes to ideas for using flax in your diet. You should also follow the instructions and ideas for making flax as a substitute in recipes that you already use or are thinking of trying. As with all substitutions they don't always give the same results as the thing you are substituting. Flax gel isn't exactly the same as eggs and as a result you need to be aware of its limitations and to a certain extent put up with them. As with all recipes the ones given here aren't set in stone, and as a result you should be prepared to adjust them according to your needs. This may involve changing the quantities used, adding extra ingredients, cutting out problem ingredients and above all experimenting. Whatever your focus, flax seeds will help you to deal with the problems that you have.

About the Author

Ellen Vincent has written 2 other books. The first book complements this 'Green Smoothie Recipes' book because it gives more of the background as to why green smoothies are so healthy and how to make them. The second book details the health benefits of Apple cider vinegar. Both books are published as paperbacks and on the kindle platform.

Green smoothies are very popular when it comes to dieting, detoxifying and giving the human body the nutrients that it needs in order to work at the peak of performance. This book explains the many ways that green smoothies can help your body and improve your health and life in general. There are plenty of tips on producing and tailoring green smoothies for your individual needs and there are over 100 exciting recipe ideas included in the book.

Green Smoothie

Diet, Detox and Recipes

Ellen Vincent

Green smoothies give you all of your nutrients the way that nature intended. This means that they are all in their raw form without chemicals, additives and processing. In basic terms you get more out your food when it is consumed in this way. This is because raw food contains more vital nutrients such as vitamins, antioxidants and amino acids. These are so good for your body that people who start eating them can experience a natural high as they are rapidly used up and turned into valuable materials. This means that green smoothies make you feel good as well as doing good.

Green smoothies are a valuable tool when it comes to dieting and losing weight. Due to the fact that they can make you feel fuller for longer they can help you to rapidly lose weight. They can also be the answer to the dieting plateau that many people reach on a normal low calorie diet. There are many other ways that green smoothies can enhance a diet or help in losing weight.

Green Smoothies could be your body's answer to those niggling health problems that can make life a misery. Modern life itself can have a bad effect on the human body and that includes the food that we eat. In seems that the further that we get away from nature, the more problems that we appear to have. If you look back to our ancestors they didn't have supermarkets and chemical additives to preserve and enhance the flavours and appearance of the foods they ate. You have to ask yourself how much damage all of these chemical additives cause? In addition to this even cooking foods causes chemical changes to happen to food and this can result in substances forming which can be bad for us and can even cause certain cancers.

If you feel like life is getting on top of you after too many 'little indulgencies' then green smoothies can be used as a way of detoxifying the body and rapidly returning it to normality.

Green Smoothie provides you with all of the information that you need to get your body working as nature intended. Get the book and join in this exciting new world of health.

Apple Cider Vinegar for Natural Health

Apple cider vinegar benefits and apple cider vinegar uses including apple cider vinegar weight loss, apple cider vinegar cures and apple cider vinegar acne

Ellen Vincent

Apple cider vinegar for natural health is all about how you can use this wonderful natural health tonic to improve your life. Apple cider vinegar has been used for centuries to treat a whole host of illnesses and conditions. These cures and remedies have become part of our folklore, but that doesn't mean that we shouldn't take them seriously. Apple cider vinegar contains many health giving substances such as vitamins, minerals, antioxidants, bioflavenoids and of course the main ingredient of acetic acid. All of these things can help our bodies to work to the peak of performance and shrug off some of those day to day conditions that get us down. You can drink apple cider vinegar or apply it directly to the skin or hair. Either way you are getting the benefit of all of these super nutrients. Some books on apple cider vinegar are written by the people who are then trying to sell the vinegar to you. I am not involved in selling these products at all. My main interest comes from my scientific and educational background together with the fact that I use apple cider vinegar myself on many occasions during my day to day life. I am a real fan and take a daily tonic to ward off illness. I also use it on my skin and hair to great effect. I am so impressed with the results that I get with apple cider vinegar that I felt compelled to research it further and then write this book. I have never come across one single substance with so many uses before, and the results can often be stunning. So, take while and look at the information in the book and then try apple cider vinegar for yourself. Pretty soon you could become a real fan too!

This version 2 of the book contains extra information, and in particular details about how to use apple cider vinegar in your daily cooking. There are plenty of recipes and cookery ideas that you can try out for yourself.

Printed in Great Britain
by Amazon.co.uk, Ltd.,
Marston Gate.